Measuring National Power

Gregory F. Treverton, Seth G. Jones

RAND NATIONAL SECURITY RESEARCH DIVISION

The proceedings described in this report were hosted by the RAND National Security Research Division, which conducts research and analysis for the Office of the Secretary of Defense, the Joint Staff, the Unified Commands, the defense agencies, the Department of the Navy, the U.S. intelligence community, allied foreign governments, and foundations.

ISBN: 0-8330-3798-6

The RAND Corporation is a nonprofit research organization providing objective analysis and effective solutions that address the challenges facing the public and private sectors around the world. RAND's publications do not necessarily reflect the opinions of its research clients and sponsors.

RAND® is a registered trademark.

Published 2005 by the RAND Corporation
1776 Main Street, P.O. Box 2138, Santa Monica, CA 90407-2138
1200 South Hayes Street, Arlington, VA 22202-5050
201 North Craig Street, Suite 202, Pittsburgh, PA 15213-1516
RAND URL: http://www.rand.org/
To order RAND documents or to obtain additional information, contact
Distribution Services: Telephone: (310) 451-7002;
Fax: (310) 451-6915; Email: order@rand.org

Preface

Understanding the nature and force of power long has been central to the study of international relations and to the work of the U.S. intelligence community. This elusive task is now all the more important because the United States enjoys an unprecedented amount of economic, military, and technological might in comparison to other states. Yet it must exercise its power in a world not only of state-related constraints on that power but also of transnational forces and non-state actors (NSAs) that act as competitors, qualifiers, constrainers, and, sometimes, enhancers of that power.

This report summarizes and extends the results of a two-day workshop the RAND Corporation hosted with the CIA's Strategic Assessments Group (SAG), in cooperation with Barry Hughes and his International Futures (IFs) model. That workshop brought together a diverse group of modelers, specialists in international relations, and thinkers about power from both the public and the private sectors. The lead presentations on the first day were by Paul Herman of the SAG, Barry Hughes, and Ashley Tellis of the Carnegie Endowment for International Peace. On the second day, the opening remarks were delivered by Jessica Mathews, president of the Carnegie Endowment, Nathan Gardels, editor, *New Perspectives Quarterly,* and editor-in-chief, Global Editorial Services, Los Angeles Times Syndicate/Tribune Media; and the Chief of the SAG. We appreciate the time and effort of those experts, many of whom we consulted more than once. Needless to say, though, we hold these good people blameless for any shortcomings that remain.

This research was conducted within the Intelligence Policy Center (IPC) of the RAND National Security Research Division (NSRD). NSRD conducts research and analysis for the Office of the Secretary of Defense, the Joint Staff, the Unified Commands, the defense agencies, the Department of the Navy, the U.S. Intelligence Community, allied foreign governments, and foundations. Comments are more than welcome. The principal author can be reached by email at Greg_Treverton@rand.org. He is also the acting director of the Intelligence Policy Center. For more information about the Center, please contact him by email, or by phone at 310-393-0411, extension 7122. More information about RAND is available at www.rand.org.

Contents

Figures and Table

Figures

Table

Summary

At the dawn of the 21st century, the concept of power is more important than ever and also more debated. How to measure the power of the United States is fundamental to the major debates over American foreign policy. If, as the globe's unipolar power, the United States has power beyond precedent, then its foreign policy problem is simplified, because friends and allies will have to follow it whether they like it or not and would-be adversaries will be cowed by the prospect of that power.

If, on the other hand, that power is less than sometimes assumed or less usable than hoped, the United States may face the prospect that erstwhile allies and friends will, almost as a law of physics, want to see it taken down a peg. They will, if not balance against it, then at least sit on the fence in circumstances like Iraq. They will be inclined to view the United States' travails with a certain *Schadenfreude,* happy to see its dominant power reduced to a more normal size but prepared to stand with the United States if it were in serious trouble.

Measuring State Power

State power can be conceived at three levels: (1) resources or capabilities, or power-in-being; (2) how that power is converted through national processes; (3) and power in outcomes, or which state prevails in particular circumstances. The starting point for thinking about—and developing metrics for—national power is to view states as "capability containers." Yet those capabilities—demographic, economic, technological, and the like—only become manifest through a process of conversion. States need to convert material resources into more usable instruments, such as combat proficiency. In the end, however, what policymakers care most about is not power as capability or power-in-being as converted through national ethos, politics, and social cohesion. They care about power in *outcomes.* That third level is by far the most elusive, for it is contingent and relative. It depends on power for what, and against whom.

The first day of the workshop concentrated on the first two levels: material capabilities and conversion. The main categories of capabilities in the Strategic Assessments Group assessment of power are gross domestic product (GDP), population, defense spending, and a less precise factor capturing innovation in technology. In the SAG estimate, the United States is first but hardly the only power. The United States holds about 20 percent of total global power, and the European Union (EU) (considered as a unified actor) and China about 14 percent each. India holds about 9 percent; Brazil, South Korea, and Russia hold about 2 percent each. Moving toward 2015, the United States will first gain power, then decline somewhat, ending up at about where it is now. The EU, however, will lose power, as will all non-U.S. members of the G-8. The gainers will be China and India.

The assessment suggests possible alliances that could match the power of the United States acting alone or with its traditional allies. It also examines the most likely locations for future conflict, based on six criteria. Asia is by far the most dangerous region, with six of the eight most conflict-prone bilateral balances involving China. The IFs model on which the SAG assessment is based is state-centric. It has data for 164 countries. As Figure S.1 summarizes, it uses eight blocks of drivers: domestic sociopolitical, international political, population, economic, agricultural, energy, technology, and environmental resources.

The work of Ashley Tellis and his colleagues examines how national resources or capabilities are transformed or converted through state processes into more usable power, in particular military power. The Tellis approach is still one of material capabilities, though it gets to what might be called *power-in-being*. It is about usable power, although it stops short of power as the abilities to achieve particular outcomes in particular circumstances. It probes beyond states as "containers of capability" to look at ideas, organization, and politics. The actual process of applying the framework to states is very data intensive, so it is important to focus on a handful of the most critical factors.

Figure S.1
Drivers of National Power

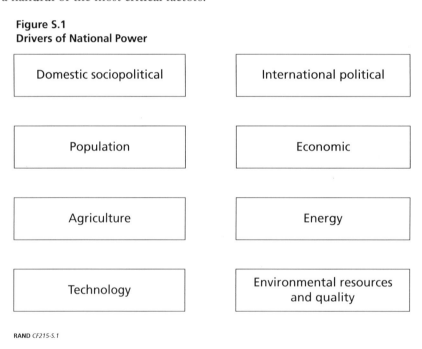

RAND *CF215-S.1*

Assessing Non-State Actors and "Softer" Forms of Power

The second day focused on the changing state system. The most obvious change is that states now have more competitors, named by what they are not—*non-state actors* (NSAs). They range from terrorists and drug traffickers to advocacy groups, think tanks, and private corporations. Those groups, and the transnational forces they create, then become the framework within which state power must be exercised. Sometimes, as with World Bank prescriptions for poorer nations, the exercise of these transnational forces is quite direct and raises questions about the differential vulnerability of states to those forces. Other transnational forces are values; they may be less easily manipulated by any actor but also may have differential impact on states: for example, a new "wave of democracy" could be important for Syria but would not have much effect on Denmark.

The traditional distinction between hard power and soft power is not entirely persuasive. For one thing, economic power might be thought of by the United States as softer than military alternatives but still be regarded as hard by the recipient. More important, the language tends to regard soft power as subordinate and second-best, whereas in fact policymakers would prefer to achieve their desired outcomes with soft power. If state power ranges from coercion to bribery to persuasion, then the last is the most cost effective; it means convincing others that your aim is also theirs. Imagine, instead, a continuum ranging from *ideal* power (persuasion) to *worst-case* power (military).

Measuring softer forms of power is no mean feat, though some metrics are available—for instance, university attendance by foreigners, or content analysis of media. One direct way of making comparisons across states might be to ask the question: Where would you live if not in your own country? Looking at cases is an indirect way to understand softer forms of power. The recent treaty banning land mines was a remarkable confluence of NSAs acting in concert with medium-sized powers. The NSAs controlled the agenda, setting both the terms of and the deadline for a treaty. Another indirect way to measure the influence of NSAs is by looking at trends, of which all six seem to contribute to redistributing power away from states and toward NSAs:

- *Access to information.* The government monopoly eroded.
- *Speed of reaction.* Markets react in seconds, but governments are much slower, so the information technology (IT) revolution inevitably moved action away from governments toward nimbler organizations.
- *New voices.* The process created new channels of information and new, credible voices. The loudest voice, that of government, became less dominant.
- *Cheaper consultation.* Because of nearly unlimited bandwidth, communication costs began to approach zero. Coordinating large and physically separated groups became much cheaper.
- *Rapid change.* Governments, by nature, are more likely to sustain the status quo than drive change, and so NSAs are often the drivers by default.
- *Changed boundaries in time and space.* IT again is driving the change, just as the invention of the printing press undermined the church's role as broker between people and their God.

According to one provocative argument, the soft power of the United States peaked after the fall of the Soviet Union when, in a quite real way, "entertainment—the power of ideas as spread by the media—finished the job of containment." Now, however, the backlash, especially in the Muslim world, is not just a reaction to U.S. policies. To those for whom life centers on faith, America appears immodest and materialistic. It is not easy for the United States to do much about that backlash.

When, moreover, the United States acts like a "normal" power, it breaks the consensus on which soft power depends. For the unipolar power to act not only unilaterally but also as a normal power—that is, only in its own interest—is, by definition, to undermine the basis of the consensual hegemony granted to it by others who expect it to look after their interests as well. Now, the "other superpower" is not a state but global public opinion, and Nelson Mandela can be regarded as the leader of that superpower. For example, in the contest

xii Measuring National Power

for "whose story wins?" at Abu Ghraib, soft power topped hard power, and the United States was demoted from hegemon to preponderant power.

Next steps for RAND, the SAG, and the International Futures model will be to strengthen the International Futures data set by adding relevant variables; to improve the formulation for forecasting power; to enhance the model foundations for forecasting power; and to develop scenarios as a means of adding vividness and exploring discontinuities.

CHAPTER ONE

Framing the Issues

The goals of the workshop were twofold: (1) to examine in detail the attributes of, and metrics for, understanding national power; and (2) to push beyond national power to the force and implications of non-state actors, transnational forces, and what is usually called *soft power*. The starting point was a confluence of recent work by both the Strategic Assessments Group and RAND, and their cooperation with Barry Hughes and his International Futures (IFs) model. The first day of the workshop focused on states and on what is customarily called *hard power*—population, technology, economics, and military might. The second day shifted attention to the role of non-state actors (NSAs) and forces, and to what are usually called the softer elements of power—ideas and culture.

State power can be conceived at three levels: (1) resources or capabilities, or power-in-being; (2) how that power is converted through national processes; (3) and power in outcomes, or which state prevails in particular circumstances. The starting point for thinking about, and developing metrics for, national power is to view states as "capability containers." Yet those capabilities—demographic, economic, technological, and the like—only become manifest through a process of conversion. States need to convert material resources, or economic prowess, into more usable instruments, such as combat proficiency. In the end, however, what policymakers care most about is not power as capability or power-in-being. They care about power in *outcomes*. That third level is by far the most elusive, for it is contingent and relative. It depends on power for what, and against whom.

The first day of the workshop concentrated on material capabilities and conversion. The second day examined some of the forces and constraints through which state power must be exercised. Of particular interest were the roles of transnational actors, ranging from international organizations to drug traffickers, and the influence of ideas and culture.

With regard to capabilities, the Strategic Assessments Group (SAG) recently published a classified study forecasting the likely structure of the international system in 2015. That study develops a sophisticated and provocative set of rankings of national power. That work attempts to fuse macro-level economic, military, demographic, and technological factors into a summary measure. Its recent publication was greeted with great interest by Washington policymakers, including at the most senior level.

The report grew out of SAG collaboration with Barry Hughes, who developed the International Futures modeling system. It is intended to serve as a thinking tool for the analysis of long-term country-specific, regional, and global futures across multiple, interacting issue areas. IFs is heavily data-rich. It represents major agent-classes (households, governments, firms) interacting in a variety of global structures (demographic, economic, social, and environmental). Hughes broke IFs into its three parts: foundations and characteristics of the power measure, strengths of that measure, and its known weaknesses.

With regard to performance or conversion, Ashley Tellis and his RAND colleagues, in *Measuring National Power in the Postindustrial Age* (MR-1110-A, 2000), argue that appreciating the true basis of national power now requires not merely a meticulous detailing of visible military assets but also a scrutiny of such factors as the aptitude for innovation, the soundness of social institutions, and the quality of the knowledge base. All of these factors may bear upon a country's capacity to produce not only effective military power but also a full quiver of national power instruments. The framework measures three distinct areas: national resources, national performance, and military capability. It then elaborates on the rationale for assessing each of these areas and offers ideas on how to measure them in tangible ways.

Breakout group assignments were made in advance. For the first day, participants were divided into three groups—one each on strategic resources, conversion, and power instruments—and were given relatively precise tasks. The first group was to identify three key strategic resources; frame an ideal indicator for each, even if that indicator is not readily at hand or measurable; and come up with its most recommended indicator. The second was to examine how conversion differs across states and what causes those differences. For instance, is conversion different for security-scarce states, like Taiwan, than for more secure ones? Again, what would be the most recommended indicator? The third group was asked, since power instruments reflect policy choices, how might that menu of choice differ in 2020 from now? What might be on the menu in the future that is not now? And again, how might that list differ between security scarce and more secure states?

The second day focused on the changing state system. The most obvious change is that states now have more competitors, named by what they are not—*non-state actors*. They range from terrorists and drug traffickers to advocacy groups, think tanks, and private corporations. One of the principal investigators wrote, "Each of the ten largest corporations in the world has a yearly turnover larger than the GNPs of 150 of 185 United Nations (UN) members, including such countries as Portugal, Israel, and Malaysia. More subjectively, at least 50 NGOs have more legitimacy than 50 UN member nations."[1] Yet how should those actors' power be conceived, let alone measured? As a first cut, might the state framework of strategic resources, conversion, and power instruments be useful, even if the items in that framework were very different—members, not armies; legitimacy, not foreign aid?

Again, breakout group assignments were made in advance, one each on the topics of the three morning sessions. Again, the groups were given relatively precise tasks. The first began to sketch a framework for defining the power of non-state actors, either on the basis of the framework of strategic resources, conversion, and power instruments or in some other way. The second examined how states will respond to transnational forces. It developed a typology of states and then considered what outcome is likely to result when a particular type of state confronts a given transnational force. The third sought to identify the three key elements of soft power; frame the ideal indicator of a nation's soft power, even if that indicator is not readily at hand or measurable; and then come up with its most recommended indicator. While the United States was the focus of the conversation, the effort to develop indicators of softer forms of power was global.

---

[1] Gregory F. Treverton, *Reshaping National Intelligence for an Age of Information* (Cambridge: Cambridge University Press, 2001), p. 49.

CHAPTER TWO

Measuring State Power

Measuring power matters directly in today's American policy debates. If the United States is really the unipolar state, one that is preponderant almost beyond historical analogy, then its policy problem is simplified. Other nations will have little choice but to follow it, whether they like it or not. They will be like Canada in the famous saying attributed to former Prime Minister Lester Pearson: "The United States is our best friend, whether we like it or not." On the other hand, if the United States is less dominant, then a national security strategy based on preponderance—on the assumption that all the major powers will be on America's side—may not hold true. What if other nations begin to align themselves not *with* the United States but *against* it, or at least hedge their bets?

Capabilities and How to Measure Them

The main metrics of world power used in the SAG assessment are gross domestic product (GDP), population, defense spending, and a less precise factor that includes innovation in technology. Power is summed as a percentage of total global power: Fourteen nations hold at least a 1 percent share. The United States holds about 20 percent of global power; the European Union (considered as a unified actor) and China, about 14 percent each. India holds about 9 percent. Brazil, South Korea, and Russia hold about 2 percent each. In moving toward 2015, the United States will first gain power, then decline somewhat, ending up at about where it is now. The EU, however, will lose power, as will all non-U.S. members of the G-8. The gainers will be China and India.

The assessment identifies possible alliances that could match the power of the United States acting alone or with its traditional allies. It also examines the most likely locations for future conflict. Asia is by far the most dangerous region, with six of the eight conflict-prone bilateral balances involving China. The IFs model on which the SAG assessment is based is state-centric. It contains data for 164 countries. As Figure 1 summarizes, it uses eight blocks of drivers: domestic sociopolitical; international political; population; economic; agricultural; energy; technology; and environmental resources.

Figure 1
Drivers of National Power

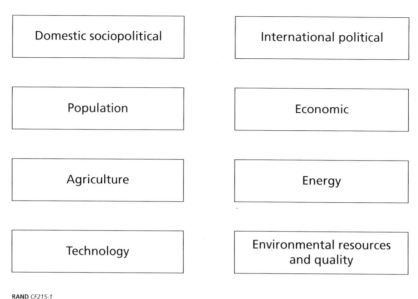

RAND *CF215-1*

Conversion, Performance, or Transformation

Ashley Tellis and his RAND colleagues offered a reexamination of the concept of national power. They began by assuming that to understand the true basis of national power requires not merely a meticulous detailing of visible military assets. It also requires a scrutiny of capabilities embodied in such variables as the aptitude for innovation, the nature of social institutions, and the quality of the knowledge base. For Tellis and colleagues, all these factors influence a country's capacity to produce the one element that is still fundamental to international politics—effective military power.

Their core argument is that national power is divided into three interlinked realms: (1) natural resources, (2) national performance, and (3) military capabilities. The first realm encompasses the level of resources either available to, or produced by, a country. The second realm encompasses national performance. It is derived from the external pressures facing a country and the efficiency of its governing institutions (nominally labeled the "state") and its society at large. The third realm encompasses military capability, which is understood in terms of operational proficiency or effectiveness. Military capability is produced as a result of both the strategic resources available to a military organization and its ability to convert those resources into effective coercive power. These three realms taken together describe national power.

The Tellis approach is still one of material capabilities, though it gets to what might be called power-in-being. It is about usable power, though not about outcomes. It drills down from states as containers of capability to look at ideas, organization, and politics. Its ultimate objective is to understand the process by which national resources are converted into military capabilities—especially capabilities that will improve combat proficiency. Tellis' approach can be applied to any country, and his team applied the analysis to China. But since the exercise can easily be overwhelmed by data, it is imperative at a macro level to focus on the three or four most critical factors. The interplay of power resources, transformative capabilities, and outcomes dominated the discussion.

Breakout Groups

Strategic Resources

The first group's objective was to find variables that help identify the great powers in the international system in 2020. The most important variables include population, human capital, economic power, technological prowess, and military capabilities. The group argued that the single most important form of power in 2020 will continue to be military power. The best single indicator of military power is the defense budget. Other indicators might include expenditures on various areas of the military, such as ground, air, and naval forces. However, these quantitative indicators do not always correlate well with military effectiveness. History demonstrates that smaller armies have defeated larger opponents because of better training, doctrine, and strategy.

Economic power is the foundation of military power. The most important single indicator is GDP. Like defense budgets, however, GDP provides only a limited picture of power. It says little about the composition of the economy, such as whether it is spearheaded by leading sectors or dominated by old and declining ones. Other important variables include human capital and technology. The best readily available measure of human capital is the average year of educational attainment. For technology, the best indicator is per-capita expenditure on research and development.

Ultimately, however, none of these indicators provides a complete picture of power in 2020. Articulating an ideal indicator is difficult, perhaps impossible. But it is likely to have something to do with *quality:* the ability of states to convert these components into outputs and make use of them. For example, is there a sense of unity and purpose in the state to mobilize and pursue national ambitions?

Converting Resources into Power

The second group examined how states translate resources into power. The group argued that while many of the issues explored by Tellis and his colleagues were critical, there is still a need to think about broadening the scope of indicators. In general, four areas are important for power conversion.

The first area encompasses economic issues, including access to capital. Researchers have generally focused on domestic economic resources and capabilities. However, changes in the global economy have created an impetus to find new indicators that measure the ability of states to utilize global resources for domestic activities. One example might be outsourcing domestic jobs to companies in foreign countries. A second area includes a state's institutions and political structures. Important indicators include the level of corruption and the size of the "selectorate": What is the size of the group to which a leader actually is accountable? This indicator matters because it affects the ability of states to allocate resources.

A third area incorporates values, trust, social capital, and other aspects of civil society. How do people cooperate and interact in political and economic relationships? To measure this, one might explore the World Values Survey and look at community organization, volunteering, and newspaper readership. The final area is social structure. This includes such aspects as societal stratification, and ethnic and class divisions.

Instruments of Power
The third group discussed future national security threats and useful instruments to address them. It argued that future threats to the United States will be caused by a combination of economic, military, environmental, and other variables. An abbreviated list includes the following:

- Major economic changes, such as the possibility of a flattening world economy and a rise in offshoring and outsourcing
- Environmental hazards, such as global pollution
- Military threats, including terrorism
- Transnational organized crime
- Demographic changes, such as a rise in megacities, aging, and immigration
- Technological and educational challenges, such as a decline in U.S. educational dominance
- Proliferation of weapons of mass destruction (WMD)
- Ideational changes, such as a decrease in liberalism or a reverse democratic wave
- New health threats, such as SARS
- An increase in new actors, such as diasporas, "smart mobs" with advanced sensors and communications technology, and technologically savvy grievance groups.

A menu of old and new power instruments will be needed to combat these threats. Several old power instruments need to change. One is the military. In the past, the military focused on conventional and nuclear warfare. In the future, it will need to focus on countering asymmetric forces. Another traditional instrument includes economic instruments. Smarter government instruments would not stifle markets and innovation but would provide social protection to populations. A third is diplomacy. Diplomacy in the United States has traditionally been about selling the American way of life to foreign governments and populations. A better approach might be to promote local groups, institutions, and policies that are compatible with U.S. goals. For example, the U.S. government might provide assistance to groups abroad that do not explicitly support the United States, and might even oppose it, but that support ideals and policies that are in the U.S. interest. This strategy may help legitimize the United States and help it better achieve policy change through diplomacy. This would be akin to the covert U.S. support for anticommunist but left-of-center groups in Europe in the wake of World War II.

Other changes in instruments might require government reorganization. The objective would be to decrease the stovepipe tendency across and within government departments and to improve cooperation. A second change might be to establish a new relationship between the government and NSAs, which some have called "deep coalitions." A final change would be the adoption of strategic restraint. Exercising restraint in America's use of hard power abroad will decrease counterbalancing and increase regional cooperation.

CHAPTER THREE

Incorporating Non-State Actors and Forces and Soft Power into Power Calculations

The second day transitioned from national power to non-state actors and transnational values and norms. It demonstrated that familiar distinctions—for instance, between public and private or foreign and domestic—are indeed becoming more blurred, and the role of the state is changing. To be sure, nation states are not about to go away, and they will remain the core of international politics for the foreseeable future. But they exercise power around and through supranational institutions and are, in turn, affected by them and by sub- and transnational actors.

In addition to those new actors, the second change in the nature of the state system is what might be called the "Westphalian flip": The Treaty of Westphalia codified a system that was multipolar but with individual states sovereign within their domains. Now, the system is unipolar, but the states, including the unipolar United States, are permeable to transnational forces. Those forces are of two sorts, and states are differentially permeable. One set of transnational forces consists of *actors,* both legitimate (international organizations) and less legitimate (traffickers in drugs, arms, or humans).

The second set of forces is *structural:* values and norms as they come to take form in international "regimes." These forces may result at least in part from actions by nations or other actors, but they also may come to have an existence of their own. States are differentially permeable to both transnational actors and forces: a new democratic wave would bear on Syria, but not Denmark. The International Monetary Fund (IMF) has more influence with poor countries than rich ones. But what accounts for how much particular states are subject to these transnational forces? Are there important differences in permeability to legitimate actors, illegitimate ones, and structural forces?

Soft power results from what states and non-state actors do and from the structural forces in the system. Softer forms of power seem more and more important in a more connected world. Yet governments cannot readily manipulate most soft power. Regis Debray, the French leftist, long ago argued that Hollywood would be a more powerful global influence for America than the Pentagon or the CIA ever hoped to be. If he is right, that influence still comes from America in general, not from specific interests or policies of the United States. Economic power is more a facilitator of other power, especially military, than usable power in its own right. There are too many suppliers and too many investors to make unilateral sanctions much of a threat in any but the rarest of circumstances. How, then, should soft power be conceived and measured, both on its own terms and in relation to states?

The hard-soft distinction, though, is deceptive on several grounds.[1] The words tend to imply that "hard is good" and "soft is bad." Yet in practice, policymakers believe the reverse: If they can prevail through the exercise of soft power, that is much better than having to apply, for instance, military muscle. Joseph Nye emphasizes that soft power is the power of attraction, not the power of coercion. When other countries are persuaded that American ideals or policies are legitimate, indeed desirable, then the "soft power" of the United States is enhanced.

Nor is the distinction between the two very precise. Economic power, for instance, is sometimes regarded as soft and sometimes as hard. It depends on who is doing the perceiving. From the perspective of the United States, economic sanctions may be softer than military force, yet from the perspective of the target, those sanctions may look very hard indeed. Rather than hard and soft, it makes more sense to think of power along a continuum from coercion, at one end, to persuasion or attraction at the other, with bribery or economic inducements perhaps in the middle. State power is the power to coerce with threats, to induce with payments, or to attract or co-opt to do what the persuader wants.

Metrics for Non-State Actors

If power is ultimately the capacity to determine outcomes, it is often said that the capacity of NSAs to affect both international and domestic outcomes is growing. Yet measuring that effect is elusive. As always, it is tempting to measure what can easily be measured, and as a result the most important factors may be excluded. To take an example from national power, gross domestic product statistics not only undervalue unpaid work, especially that done by women, but also exclude the nation's natural resources, which have value in the national income accounts only as they contribute to producing current goods and services.

NSAs have long been active in human rights, the environment, and national resources, and they are increasingly cooperating with UN agencies. They might be thought of as existing along a continuum from pure advocacy at one end to pure service delivery at the other. Some of the largest non-government organizations, or NGOs, are churches, which are mostly at the service delivery end of the spectrum. Yet the line separating churches from what are customarily thought of as NGOs, organizations like Amnesty International, is blurred.

So how should we begin to understand, if not measure, the role and power of NSAs? One way is by looking at *cases and their outcomes*. Another is to examine *trends*. For instance, the process that led to the international treaty banning land mines broke all the usual rules. It brought together NGOs and medium-sized governments, like Canada, Australia, and Belgium. All five permanent members of the UN Security Council initially opposed the idea. But the NSAs not only put the text on the agenda at the beginning, they also set the goal and terms of the debate: "Join us or not, but we will not compromise the basic goal." And they achieved a treaty in 14 months. The keys to success were that, on the one hand, there was little money in land mines, hence weak private interests advocating on their behalf. On the

---

[1] The distinction owes most notably to Joseph S. Nye, Jr. See *The Paradox of American Power: Why the World's Only Superpower Can't Go It Alone* (New York: Oxford University Press, 2002); and *Soft Power: The Means to Success in World Politics,* (New York: Public Affairs, 2004).

other hand, a wide coalition of groups—from Vietnam veterans to health and agriculture advocates—favored a ban.

In the negotiations for a global warming framework agreement that was the precursor to the Kyoto Protocol, the medium-sized countries were again central, and the NSAs were again far out in front. Agreement was reached in a matter of months, not years. States remain key, but NSAs shape and channel the power of states. Governments can dig in, as the United States has done on global warming. But when an eventual global warming treaty is produced, it will be produced within the framework that was shaped by the Kyoto process.

A second way of conceiving the power of NSAs is to look at trends. Surely, the IT revolution, coinciding with the end of the Cold War, redistributed power away from states and toward NSAs, in at least six ways:

- *Access to information.* The government monopoly on information has eroded. In the 1980s, environmentalists became concerned about old growth forests in the northwestern United States. But how much of those forests had been lost? The government did not say. But the Wilderness Society used Landsat images to make its own estimates. That use of commercial imagery, commonplace now, was revolutionary then.
- *Speed of reaction.* Markets react in seconds, but governments are much slower, so the IT revolution inevitably moved action away from governments toward nimbler organizations.
- *New voices.* The process created new channels of information and new, credible voices. The loudest voice, that of government, became less dominant.
- *Cheaper consultation.* Because of nearly unlimited bandwidth, communication costs began to approach zero. Coordinating large and physically separated groups has become much cheaper—witness the role of ethnic diasporas in the United States.
- *Rapid change.* Governments, by nature, are more likely to sustain the status quo than drive change, and so NSAs are often the drivers by default. That was true of the civil rights movement, although the term NGO was not in use then. Rapid change, however, often has an ugly side and produces a backlash, like the violent Islamic reaction in many parts of the world today.
- *Changed boundaries in time and space.* IT again is driving the change, just as the invention of the printing press undermined the church's role as broker between people and their God. Is the state's role as broker being similarly undermined? Surely, definitions of "us" and "them" are changing, notably in Europe and the Muslim world.

In response, though, participants observed that the tug of war between states and private groups has been going on for a long time: Recall the Rothschild banks, the Masons, or the Red Cross. At the same time, the share of GNP controlled by states is generally going up, not down. NGOs are hardly new. If there is a difference now, it is one of scale. Not only are NSAs ubiquitous, but it is not necessary to be a Rothschild to get access to decisionmaking. Notice the difference between the private relief activities of the Red Cross and the land mines treaty. Red Cross activities begin and remain private. But it was governments that in the end signed the land mines treaty, and governments will enforce it. Yet to the extent that the technology for enforcing the treaty is public, individuals or non-government groups can monitor the rules directly.

NSAs have influence in a number of ways. At the extreme, a Pacific island country, Vanuatu, in effect turned over its climate delegation to a London-based NGO. With 900 climate-related treaties in existence, governments, even big ones, simply cannot manage them all. They become dependent on NGOs. In other cases, NGOs may have influence in part because they are *congruent* with the interests of important states; in that sense, what Freedom House does is congruent with U.S. interests in democracy. By contrast, NGOs are weak in Japan. Part of the reason is Japan's tax system, but the weakness goes deeper. Many NGOs are led by women, who have been excluded from the traditional corridors of power. In that sense, the weakness of the NGO sector is a mirror of deeper weaknesses in the making of Japanese policy.

In sum, four kinds of reaction or backlash to the growing role of NSAs can be identi-fied. One, especially in the richer countries, is the increased salience of security, the tradi-tional domain of states, after September 11. A second reaction, more visible in poorer coun-tries, is the growing recognition that those countries may have too little governance instead of too much. They need more legitimate authority, not less, to enforce contracts, open in-formation flows, and the like.

A third reaction, in poor countries but perhaps more so in rich ones, is based on le-gitimacy. For all their faults, governments in democracies have the legitimacy that comes with being elected. But no one elected Amnesty International. Moreover, governments are intended to develop an integrated public interest, while most NGOs have narrow or special interests. They also tend to be all-or-nothing organizations, not eager for the compromises that are the stuff of politics. American democracy is starting to display the fact that piling special interests on top of one another is not the same as integrating across them to produce a public interest.

Finally, if the middle class is in some sense a creation of the state, then a fourth backlash may derive from the changing role of the state. Governments used to control the value of their currencies but can do so no longer. They now have little control over where "their" companies locate research or production, and those companies are less and less theirs. The U.S. debate over outsourcing may be a symptom of that backlash.

The Nature of Soft Power

National borders are surely more porous now, and the nature of power itself may be chang-ing. In one direction, by 2010 a third of California's smog will come from China. In the other direction, China's border is also porous, and "Net-izens" there outnumber Communist Party members. Power now derives from economics and from the pull on hearts and minds; power, especially soft power, depends on consent. It depends on the dominant power *not* behaving as a normal state but rather taking the interests of other states into account when framing its actions.

In the latter sense, the soft power of the United States may already have peaked. In Iraq, in particular, it looked to others as though it was pursuing, if not its own unilateral in-terests, then surely its own unilateral vision. In soft power terms, the United States may al-ready have been demoted from hegemon to predominant power. Ideas defeated the Soviet Union. Debray's argument is on the mark. Or as Michael Eisner might put it, entertainment finished the job of containment. That was the high point for the "colonels of Disney." Now, there is more competition, ranging from Al Jazeera to the Chinese web.

Moreover, the backlash, especially in the Muslim world, is not just a reaction to U.S. policies. To those for whom life centers on faith, America seems immodest and materialistic. Masoumeh Ebtekar, the highest-ranking woman in the Iranian government, says that a woman covering up her body should be considered super-feminism because it frees her from sexual objectification and harassment in the workplace. The backlash also occurs within the United States, for behind the lascivious media images, the country is socially conservative.

When the United States acts not only unilaterally but also as a normal power—that is, only in its own interest—it undermines the basis of the consensual hegemony granted to it by others, who expect it to look after their interests as well. The "other superpower" is now not a state but rather global public opinion, and Nelson Mandela can be regarded as the leader of that superpower. In the contest for "whose story wins?" at Abu Ghraib, soft power topped hard power, and the United States undermined its power. It was demoted from hegemon to preponderant power. The strong school of French intellectuals who had become anti anti-American, like Jean-François Revel, were undercut.

Moreover, regaining soft power is harder than rearming. The latter takes only political will, while the other is a long march to reestablish credibility and re-win hearts and mind once lost. However, there is no visible global challenge to America's soft power at present. The Muslim reaction is not a hegemonic challenge. Nor is the appeal of China, which has replaced Japan as Asia's economic beacon; young Koreans now learn Chinese, not English.

Another perspective on soft power begins with the proposition that power is the capacity to determine outcomes. Soft power then becomes everything short of physical force; it is "preparing the battlefield." For intelligence to notice what the hundred richest people in the world are doing is to know the context in which the world operates. A common answer to the question of why the United States cannot control Iraq when Saddam Hussein could, is that it is not as ruthless as he was. Yet that does not seem satisfactory. Another part of the answer seems to be the diversification of the world away from the United States as a cultural model.

In that sense, no investor would now "buy" unipolarity. Not only are China and India on the rise economically, but military power, where the United States is most dominant, is less usable than it was before. During the Cold War, there was talk of the "Finlandization" of Europe. Now we may be seeing the "Sino-ization" of Asia. Moreover, culturally as well as economically, the world is evolving away from a hub-and-spoke arrangement with the United States as the hub.

For intelligence, this situation implies the need to think about and measure the soft power of others. Osama bin Laden has lots of soft power. Yusuf Islam (formerly Cat Stevens) is half-forgotten in the United States, but he remains popular in Malaysia. Denying him entry to the United States in 2004 was treated as a kind of joke here, but it was a serious matter—and a powerful symbol—elsewhere. Unusual metrics may bear on soft power, and normal clandestine collection is not likely to be very useful in producing information to flesh out those metrics. In Nazi Germany, for instance, soldiers' obituaries charted the decline of Hitler as a symbol; early on, those soldiers died for "Führer and Fatherland," but by war's end they mostly died for their country alone.

China and India are very different from one another. Does that difference increase or decrease their soft power? Or does the fact that they remain poor create a lag in noticing that power? In any case, they will be competitors, and information technology will be critical. They both want to take their "brand" out of the "ethnic ghetto" of hyphenation (Chinese-American or Indian-American), into the mainstream. But is cultural power good or bad? The example of the U.S. entertainment industry makes that an open question. In any case, intelligence needs to monitor the competition. One indicator would be content analysis to see which "stories" are most prevalent or most accepted. Soft power lets some countries, the Nordics for example, punch above their weight. For others, like Turkey or Austria, soft power needs to be seen in their context, not ours.

Soft power might be measured in a number of ways. The technological innovation might be tracked up and down the value chain. Nations' patterns of aid might be observed. The spread of language learning, especially of English versus Chinese, might be monitored. So might the spread of art, films, and other icons of culture; Japanese films are now "cool" when the global teenager is not necessarily American. One could ask how much the popularity of governments affects soft power. Tourism, emigration, alliance networks, and patterns of telephone and Internet communication would be other indicators. Surveys might ask "what country's products would you most like to purchase?" as an index of economic power; or "what country's news and information do you most trust?" as a measure of national integrity.

The ensuing discussion continued the debate about hard versus soft power, again recognizing that the terms are not entirely satisfactory. Soft power probably enhances the room for the weak to maneuver, giving them more opportunity to resist coercion. Still, for realists, the traditional view of the world as anarchic still holds. Realists believe that what alienates people around the world is not America's culture but rather its use of power as reflected in its policies. From an economic perspective, too, the state retains a hold—perhaps a reflection of its role in creating a middle class. People are prepared to pay higher prices for steel if protectionism safeguards U.S. jobs. When jobs are outsourced overseas, it is seen as a loss. Plainly, hard and soft power are complements in the end: Hard power destroyed the Taliban in Afghanistan and Saddam in Iraq, but exercising the softer power of consent has proven harder.

Breakout Groups

Types of Non-State Actors

The first group was charged with thinking about different types of NSAs. It developed a taxonomy that included types of non-state actors; ways to measure the power of non-state actors; and constraints on their power. It divided non-state actors into six types.

The first type includes corporations, whose power can be measured in financial resources, human capital, technology, and information. States constrain the power of corporations by exercising regulatory oversight over them. The second type incorporates NGOs and civil society, whose power can be measured by examining their influence on elites, popular opinion, and civil action. However, they are constrained because most cannot implement policy; they can only advocate it. The third type includes international organizations, such as the World Bank, IMF, World Trade Organization (WTO), and UN. The modes of power for some of these organizations, such as the World Bank and IMF, include allocating government and private financial flows. The modes of power are somewhat different for organizations like the WTO and UN, which try to build consensus for state collective action and changes in policy and the status quo.

The fourth type covers regional economic associations such as the Association of Southeast Asian Nations (ASEAN) and the EU. These groups exercise power by defining market access and working to develop consensus for state action. The fifth type of non-state actor includes terrorists and criminal cartels. These actors can wield substantial asymmetric power, based on their willingness to use violence, encourage corruption, and affect policy. The final type covers virtual networks, such as computer hackers and music-sharing groups like Kazaa. Table 1 summarizes the results of this group's discussion.

In addition to these types of non-state actors, there are also hybrid organizations. For instance, the International Organization for Standardization, which develops standards for businesses and governments, brings together states, NGOs, and private companies. Of particular interest for the intelligence community might be to ask several questions about all types: Which non-state actors have methods and objectives that run in parallel with U.S. national interests, and which against? How can the United States influence non-state actors?

Table 1
Types of Non-State Actors

Type	Modes of Action	Measures	Constraints
Private corporations	Conduct market operations	Profit, market share	States still have regulatory oversight
NGOs and civil society	Provide information and assistance	Media appearances, resources	Often single-issue organizations; can't implement policy, only advocate
International organizations	Allocate financial resources, send signals about investment possibilities	Resources, size	Little impact on powerful countries
Regional economic organizations	Accelerate economic growth through trade	Size, amount of trade	States still retain primary economic power
Terrorists and criminal cartels	Use terror, engage in illicit activity	Resources, size, global reach, capabilities	Asymmetry of power compared to states
Virtual networks, such as computer hackers	Influence ideas and views of users	Website hits, number of subscribers	No troops and hard power

Types of Transnational Actors and Forces
The second group also started with NSAs and other transnational forces. Its initial list was similar to the first group's—NGOs, international organizations, diasporas, terrorists, international criminal organizations, informal transnational coalitions, multinational corporations (MNCs), and the media. The list might be summarized in three categories defined by what the international actors seek: actors whose objective is to advocate values, norms, and policies (NGOs and intergovernment organizations); actors who try to circumvent or undermine state power (terrorists and criminals); and actors whose relationship with the state is one of convenience (MNCs).

The salient forces are nationalism, human rights, democracy and accountability, free markets, trade, demographics, globalization, and non-state governance. Others would include environment, perhaps the strongest area of international governance. The spread of nuclear capability and weapons is another, and the information revolution is also continuing to spread and develop. A simple two-by-two matrix is useful in tracing the effect of these actors and forces (Figure 2).

The horizontal axis represents a continuum from strong government to weak. The vertical axis represents regime type, which ranges from democratic to autocratic. This matrix produces four boxes: (1) a democracy with a strong government, like France; (2) a democracy with a weak state apparatus, like Mexico (the United States might also be in this category); (3) an autocratic state with a strong government, like China; and, finally, (4) a weak autocracy, for instance, Sudan.

The figure might be used to help assess state responses and vulnerabilities to particular transnational forces. Consider the impact of ethnic diasporas residing in a state. Their effect in a strong democratic state is likely to lead to conflict; the ongoing debate over head scarves for Muslim women in France is an example of that conflict. By contrast, diasporas are more likely to co-opt government policy in a weak democracy. In the United States, for example, the Cuban lobby has controlled U.S. policy toward Cuba for two generations. U.S. policy on Cuba is run from Miami. When a strong autocracy confronts a diaspora, the outcome is likely to be a strong government effort, probably successful, to eliminate the diaspora. An example would be the Soviet Union, which went to great lengths to deny ethnic minorities an independent identity. When weak autocratic states confront a diaspora, the result is likely to be civil war.

Or consider free trade as a transnational force. In a weak, democratic state, the result would be the rise of dual economies and political conflict as the informal economy grew. In a strong democracy, the likely outcome of free trade would be an effort toward managed trade.

In a strong autocracy, the result would be selective liberalization with suppression of other aspects of the neo-liberal regime—China is a good example. In a weak autocracy, the

Figure 2
Types of Transnational Actors

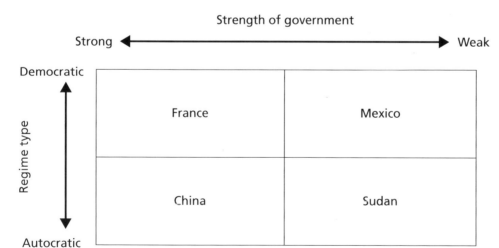

impact of free trade would be to bypass the state structure completely, which would lead to corruption and other manifestations of a breakdown in the rule of law.

Parsing Soft Power

The third group started from the premise that "soft power" was not a useful term. Instead, the range from coercion to attraction might be divided into economic, ideational, and cultural power. Indicators for the first might be foreign aid, trade partners, trade volume, and the like; for the second, university attendance by foreigners, members or adherents, contributions received, hits on websites and the like; and for the third, where foreigners choose to live or work, content analysis of media, and the like.

What is the best single indicator of a nation's power in this realm? Poll responses to the question, "where would you like to live other than your own country?" would capture some of all three dimensions and also involves some personal stake in the answer. For that reason, it may be a better question than "which country do you admire most and why?" ("Where would you least like to live?" might measure negative soft power.)

CHAPTER FOUR

Next Steps

Power is an elusive concept. As the famed political scientist Hans Morgenthau wrote, "The concept of political power poses one of the most difficult and controversial problems of political science."[1] This conference examined the attributes of national power and metrics for understanding it. The aim was to push beyond the concept of power as material capabilities and to explore the role of non-state actors, transnational forces, and what some have termed soft power. The presentations, breakout group sessions, and discussions led to several possible next steps for RAND, the Strategic Assessments Group, and the International Futures model:

- Strengthen the International Futures data set by adding relevant variables.
- Improve the formulation for forecasting power.
- Enhance the model foundations for forecasting power.
- Develop scenarios.

1. Strengthen the International Futures Data Set

The conference discussions elicited several variables and indicators that provide information about the current state of power distribution in the international system—especially in its softer forms—which might be incorporated in IFs. Particular examples include cultural attractiveness, political outcomes (such as WTO rulings), knowledge generation and use, non-state actors, governance effectiveness, and a measure for globalization.

Cultural attractiveness includes the consumption of U.S. culture; the prevalence of English; the spread of U.S.-style institutions; and the attractiveness of U.S. universities. It would be interesting to find or develop an opinion poll that asked respondents the question about softer forms of power that seemed to participants to be the best indicator: If you could live anywhere in the world other than in your own country, where would you live and why? Would you choose because of economic, political, cultural, or other reasons?

A second set of indicators is political outcomes, such as UN votes and WTO dispute rulings. Which states win and which lose? A third would frame knowledge generation and use. This includes a variety of research and development expenditures (total amounts, basic research levels, military research levels); the extent of education at the college level and be-

---

[1] Hans J. Morgenthau, *Politics Among Nations: The Struggle for Power and Peace*, Third Edition (New York: Alfred A. Knopf, 1963), p. 27.

yond; quality of education; and knowledge infrastructure, such as computers, telephones, networked users. Fourth is the growth and influence of non-state actors, such as NGOs. Fifth is a variable for "governance effectiveness," perhaps tied to the World Bank Indicators of Governance and Institutional Quality data set. A composite governance indicator might include a governance effectiveness measure and levels of democracy, transparency, and perhaps economic freedom. A final indicator might be a measure of globalization tied to foreign direct investment flows and trade connections.

It would be useful for the Strategic Assessments Group to have these measures available for analysis. The International Futures database and analysis toolkit offers an obvious route to accomplishing this step. It provides basic tools for longitudinal analysis, cross-sectional analysis, and mapping. In fact, a number of measures such as those suggested above are already in the database in some form. Some logical next steps would be developing a list of additional measures desired, adding data where possible, tagging "power indicators" in the broader IFs database to facilitate bringing them up for focused analysis, and building a specialized report form for countries (and groupings) that focuses on power measures in categories yet to be developed.

2. Improve the Formulation for Forecasting Power

It might be useful to build on these variables and indicators in several ways. First, they could be linked to the set of factors from which the aggregate power index is computed. The system of flexible weighting that already exists should make this linkage relatively easy. In addition, it might be useful to create an *absolute power index*. The current power index measures relative power; states are measured as a percentage of system power.

Over time, however, many states and non-state actors have been increasing their absolute power in ways that affect overall system behavior. For instance, when non-state actors like terrorist groups achieve significant absolute power, such as the ability to do harm, that fact may be more important than their relative power, which still is likely to be modest. On the other hand, the relative power of the United States, while enormous, has limits in absolute terms—limits visible in Iraq. So some indicators or thresholds for absolute power would be helpful, particularly for U.S. intelligence.

Second, it may be useful to simplify and improve the user interface for addressing power. It might be helpful, for instance, to add a basic report capability focused on the indices of power and the component elements of it. It might also be worth considering a specialized form to simplify the controlling of weighting and index construction.

3. Enhance the Model Foundations for Forecasting Power

Forecasts are only as good as the underlying model. The model foundations could be enhanced in at least three areas. First, it would be useful to turn attention to the representation of the production function in the economic model. The quality of economic growth forecasts is fundamental to most of what the model does. It would be helpful to better represent that production function in a way that builds more extensively on current endogenous growth theory. Second, it might be helpful to develop the education submodel. Third, the representation of debt and its impact on countries needs significant work. Some significant power shifts could occur in the international system in the future as a result of exchange rate changes and financial crises.

4. Develop Scenarios

It would be extremely beneficial to develop a number of scenarios about the future of power, rather than relying only on the base case. The most obvious set of scenarios would build on different assumptions of economic growth rates. For example, RAND, which has a long tradition of developing scenarios and other ways of thinking about the future, has applied a technique called "fault lines" to China. The analysis asked what major fault lines (adversities) might seriously affect China's ability to sustain rapid economic growth. It identified such factors as unemployment, poverty, and social unrest; corruption; HIV-AIDS and epidemic disease; and water resources and pollution. It then asked how these adversities might occur, and by how much they would affect China's growth.

Wild cards—exogenous shocks to the system—are also important to consider. If the IFs model is run forward from, say, the 1960s, it does not do well at predicting what actually happened. The main reason is external shocks, such as the oil crisis of the 1970s. Future shocks might include energy system shocks, such as a dramatic increase in oil prices; financial shocks; the collapse of key regimes; or lethal new terrorist attacks. One way RAND has looked at shocks is by considering *breaking continuities,* searching for factors where predictions of continuity seem dubious, even if predicting exactly how, let alone when, that continuity might break is elusive. Such breaks seem especially likely when two measures of continuity are uneasy partners. Examples of factors identified in work on Asian futures several years ago included the following:

- *Korea:* The heavily armed confrontation is sustained; North Korea declines economically but does not collapse.
- *China-Taiwan:* Relations heat up and cool down, but the standoff continues. China does not accept de facto Taiwanese autonomy and Taiwan does not declare de jure independence.

In sum, the conference produced a number of fruitful next steps. These include strengthening the IFs data set, improving the power index, enhancing the power model's foundations, and developing future scenarios. These steps can provide policymakers with a more useful set of variables to measure power and ultimately should improve their ability to understand the future security environment.